PENGUIN BOOKS

PUNOGRAPHY

Bruce A. McMillan was born in Boston, grew up in Maine, and earned his B.S. degree in biology at the University of Maine in 1969. His varied career has already included work as a television producer-director, a television photographer, and an island caretaker—he, his wife, and their son having been the sole year-round residents of a secluded Maine island for two years. In addition to *Punography*, Mr. McMillan is the author of three photographic books for young readers: *Finestkind o' Day: Lobstering in Maine; The Alphabet Symphony,* an ABC book; and *The Remarkable Riderless Runaway Tricycle.* He lives with his family in Shapleigh, Maine.

The bookplate

PUNCG

Bruce A. McMillan

RAPHY

Penguin Books

Penguin Books Ltd, Harmondsworth,
Middlesex, England
Penguin Books, 625 Madison Avenue,
New York, New York 10022, U.S.A.
Penguin Books Australia Ltd, Ringwood,
Victoria, Australia
Penguin Books Canada Limited, 2801 John Street,
Markham, Ontario, Canada L3R 1B4
Penguin Books (N.Z.) Ltd, 182–190 Wairau Road,
Auckland 10, New Zealand

First published 1978
Reprinted 1979, 1980

Copyright © Bruce A. McMillan, 1978
All rights reserved

LIBRARY OF CONGRESS CATALOGING IN PUBLICATION DATA
McMillan, Bruce A.
  Punography
  1. American wit and humor, Pictorial.   I.   Title.
NC1429.M265A4   1978   779'.092'4   78-5174
ISBN 0 14 00.4839 1

Printed in the United States of America by
Halliday Lithograph Corporation, West Hanover, Massachusetts
Set in Helvetica

For Terry,
who, somehow,
puts up with me
when I get
consumed by
my photography,
and
for Lewis, my friend

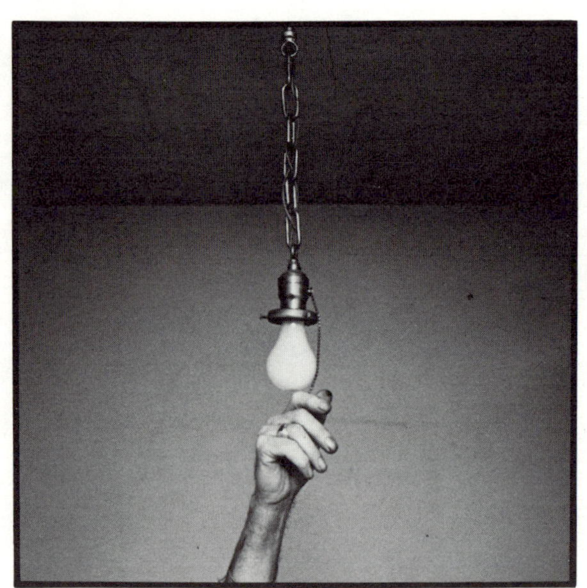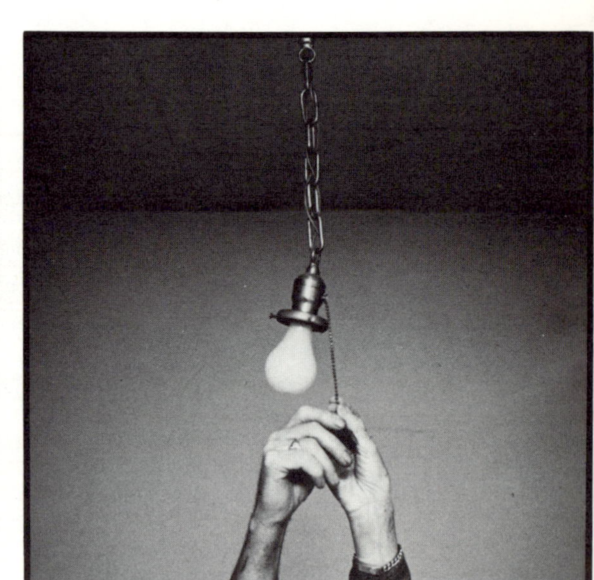

Many hands make light work.

A fork in the road

Force of habit

 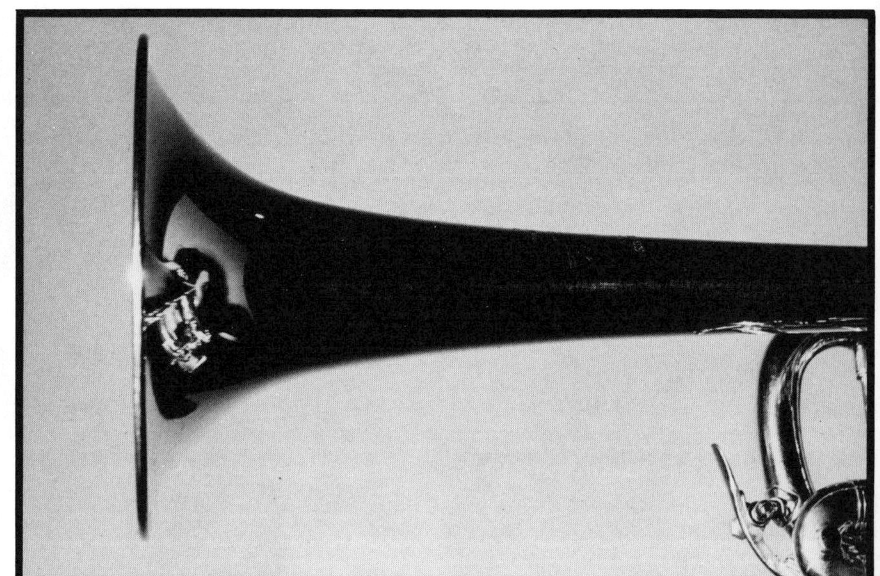

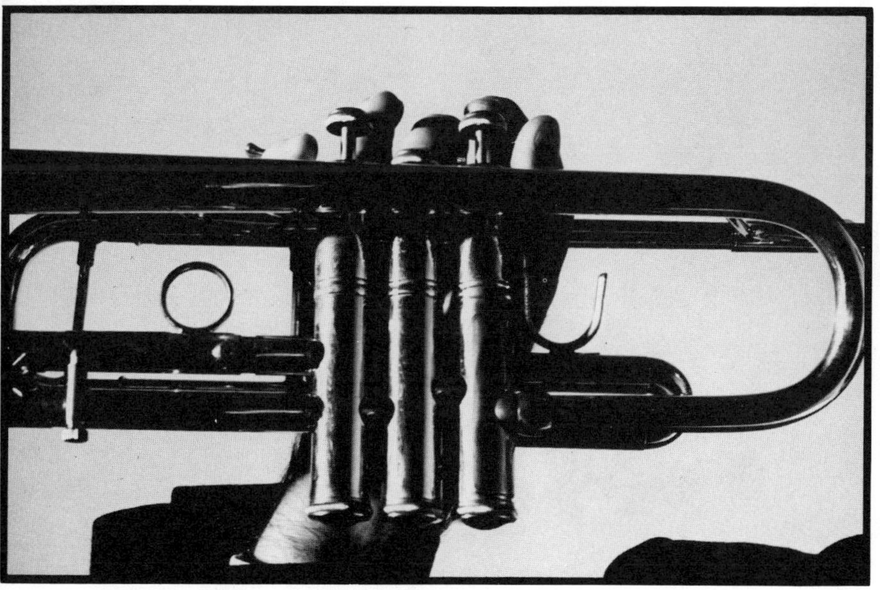

Playing it by ear

Shooting the breeze

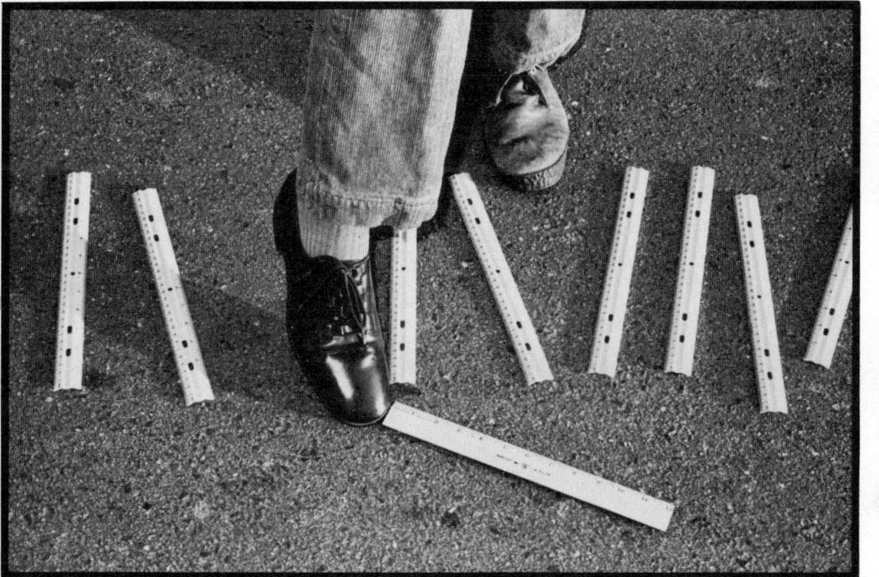

Putting your best foot forward

CABBAGE
10¢ lbs

CABBAGE
10¢ lbs

Two heads are better than one.

Hoggin' the road

A salt and battery

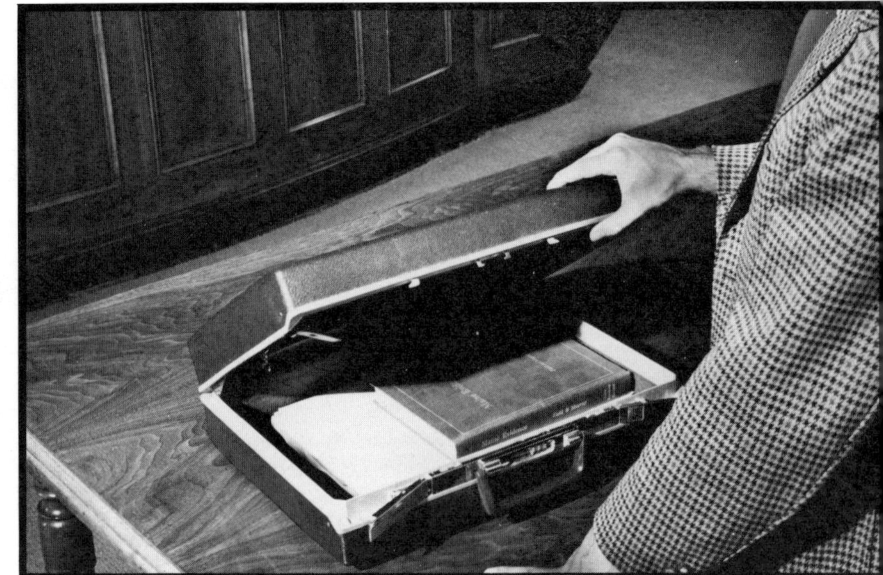

An open and shut case

People are dying to go there.

Bark up the wrong tree

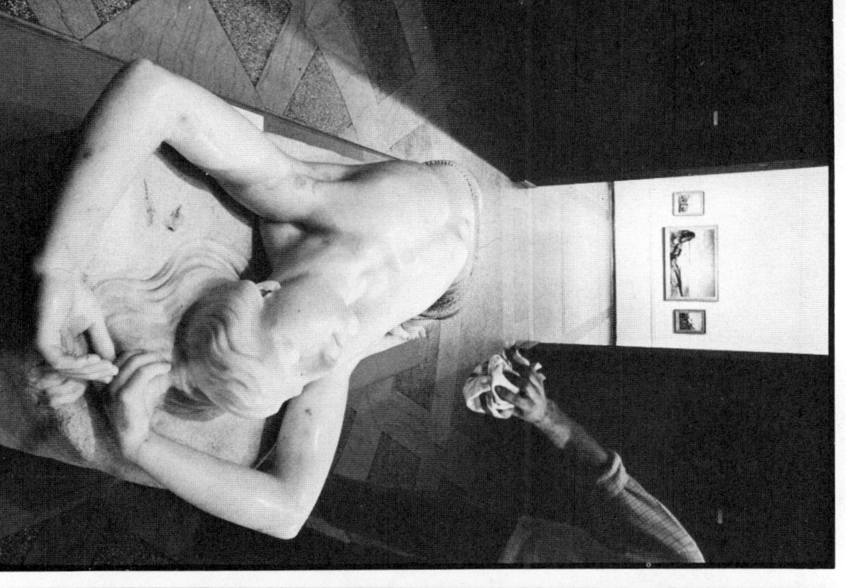
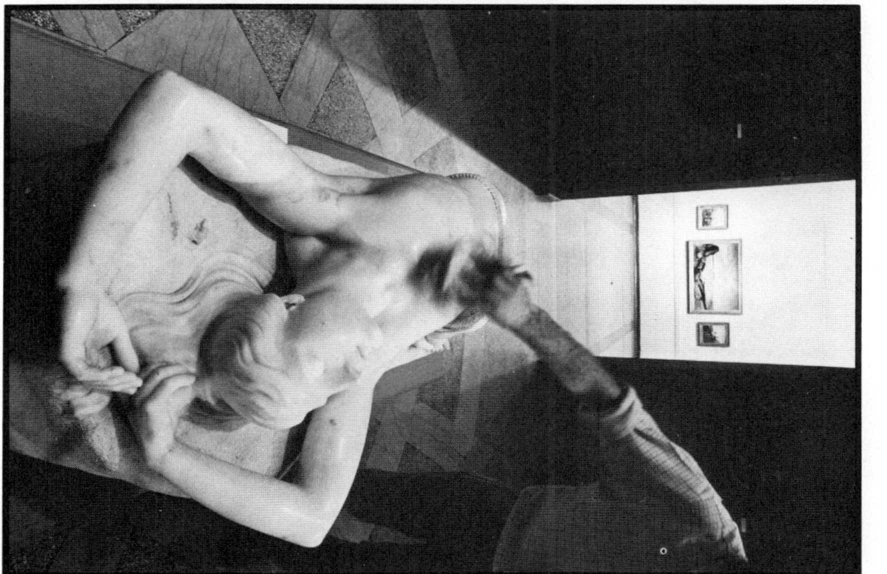

Making a clean breast of it

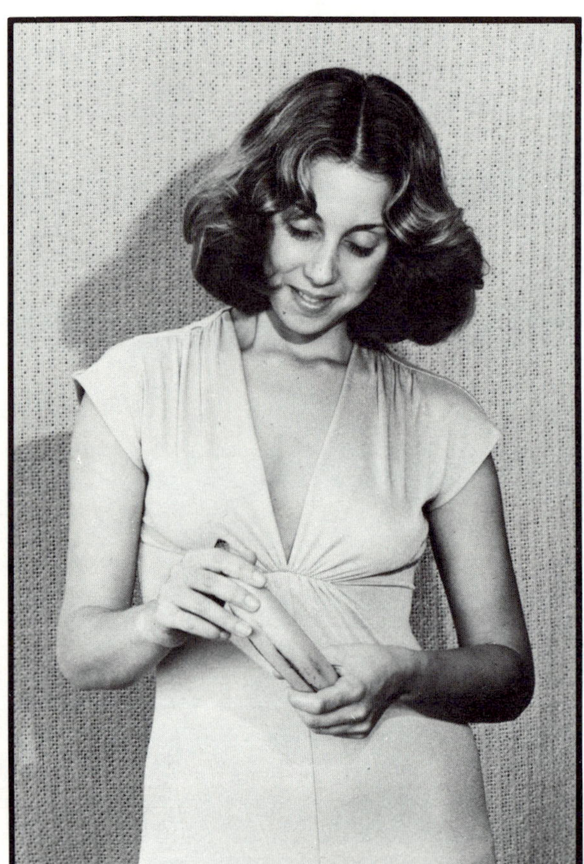

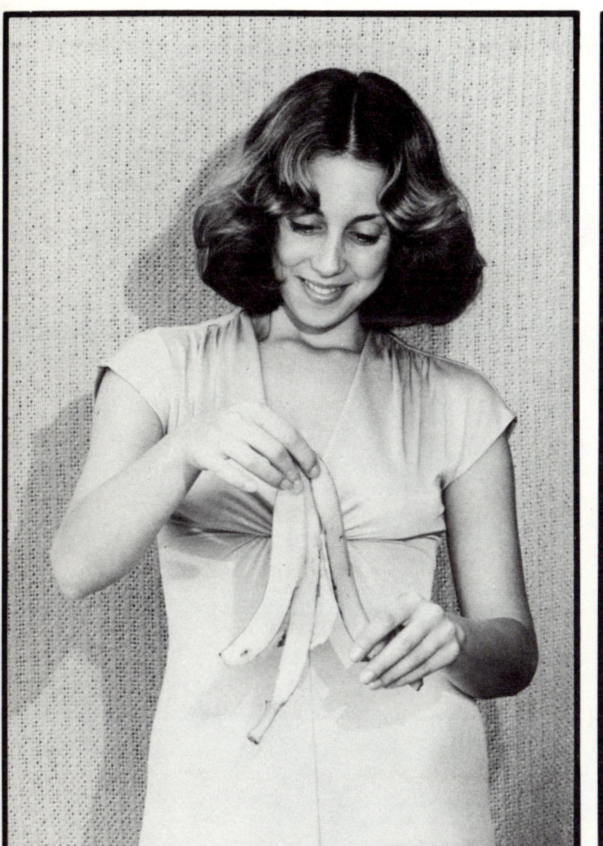

She's got a peel.

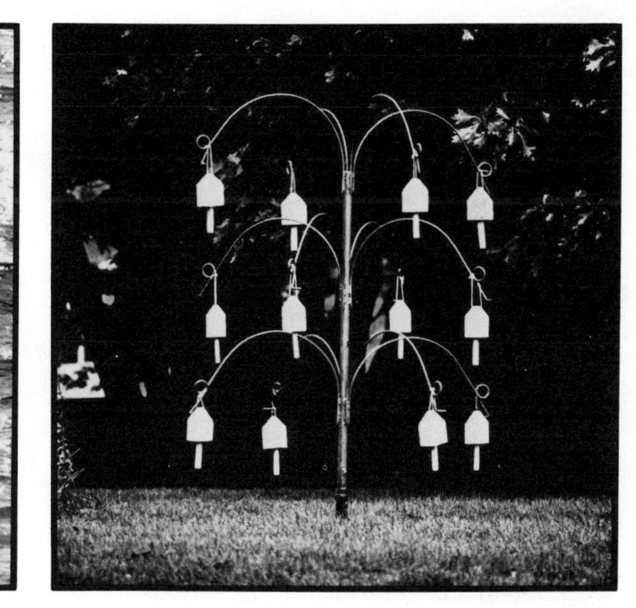

Buoys will be buoys.

A rock group getting stoned

THE
BAG

THE
BAG

THE
BAG

Half in the bag

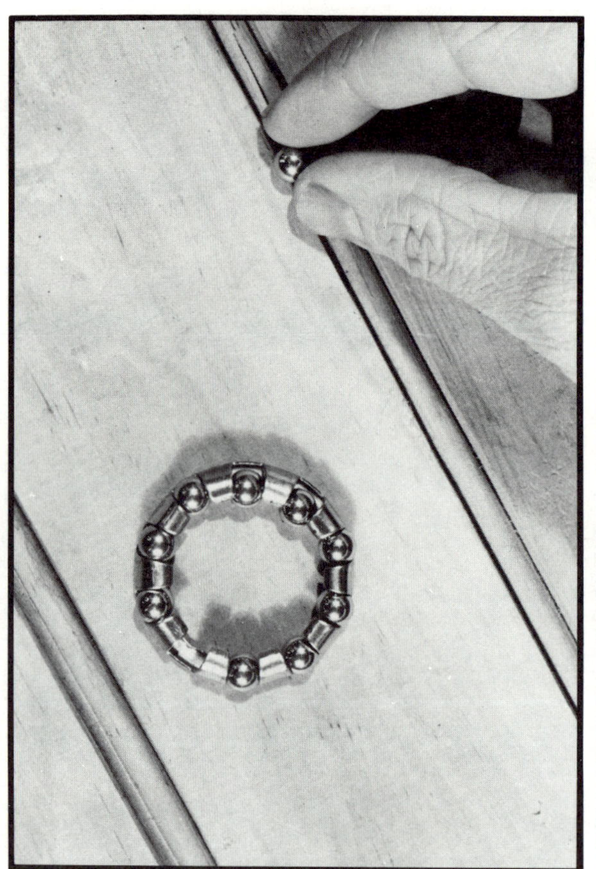
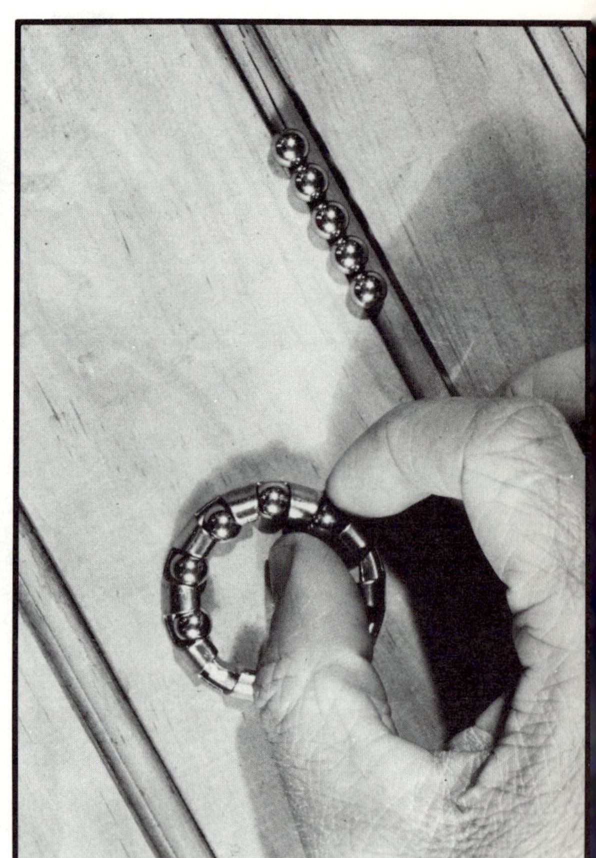

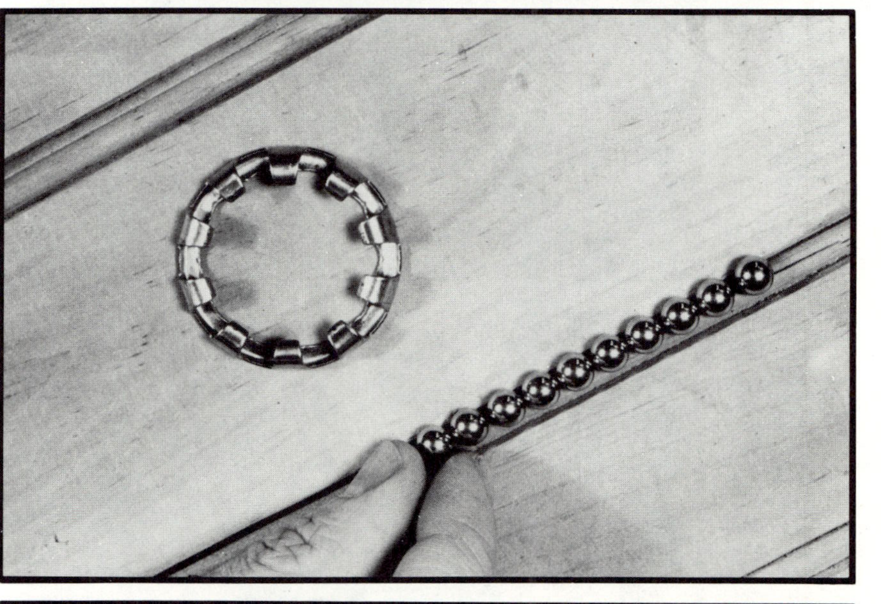
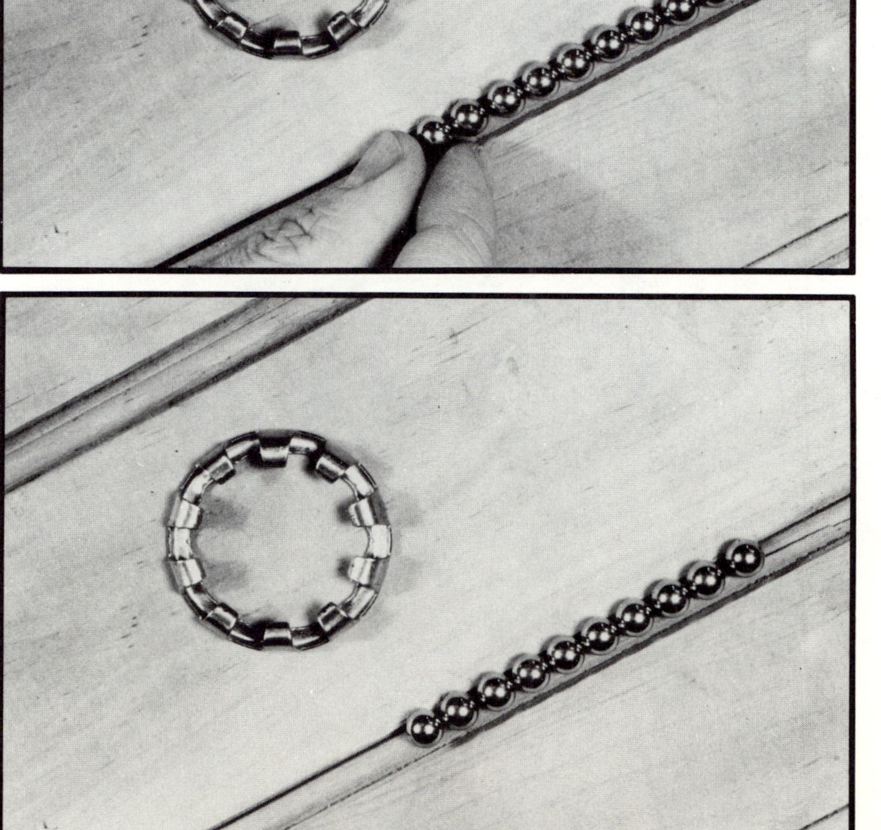

Getting your bearings straight

Nothing like being on the safe side

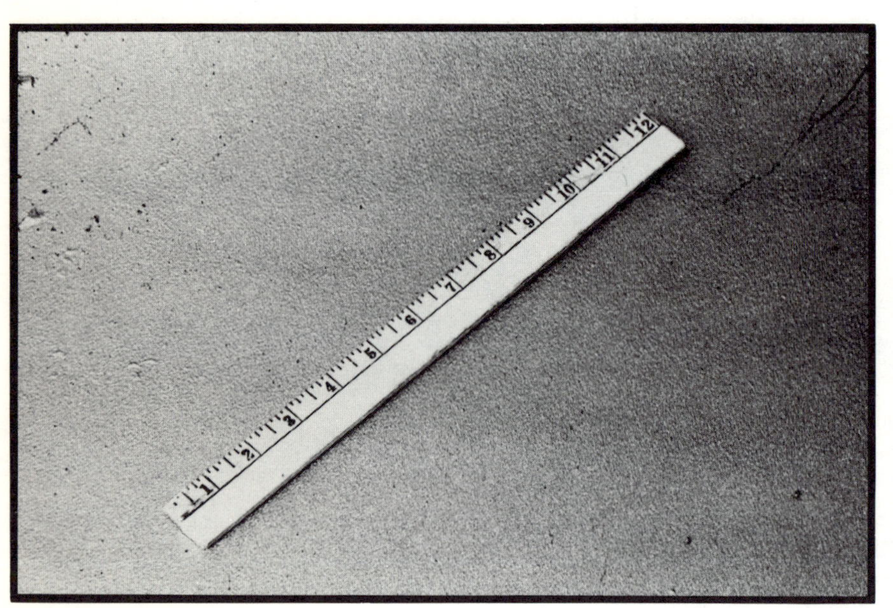

One foot in the grave

The blind leading the blind

Taking a stand

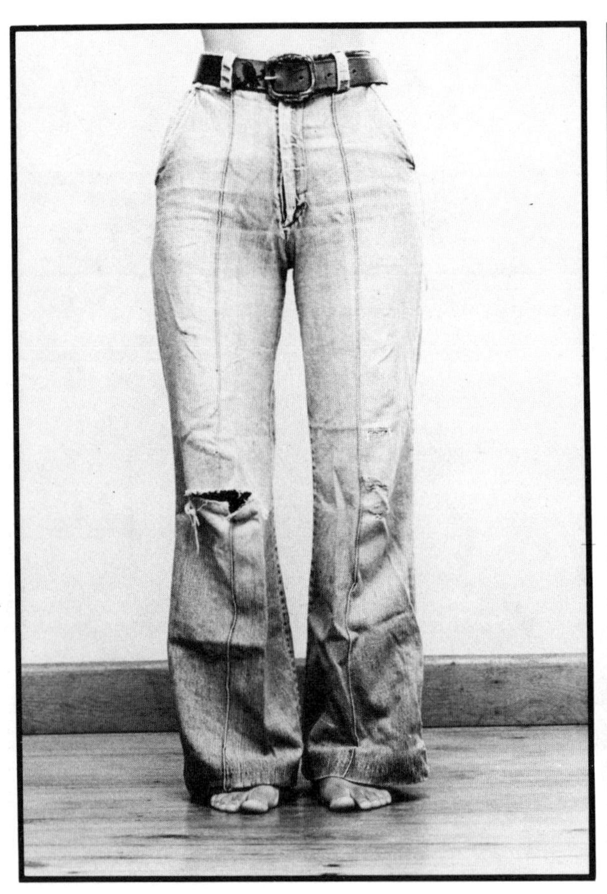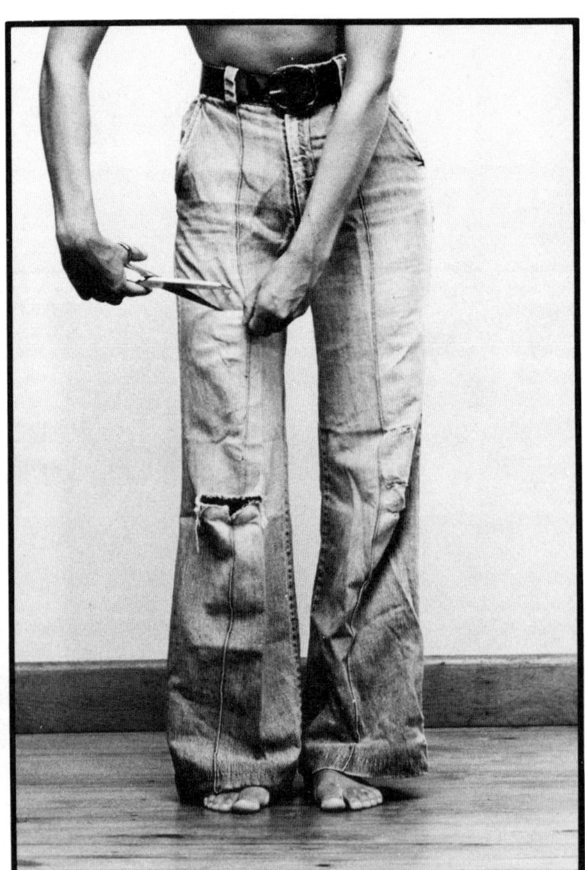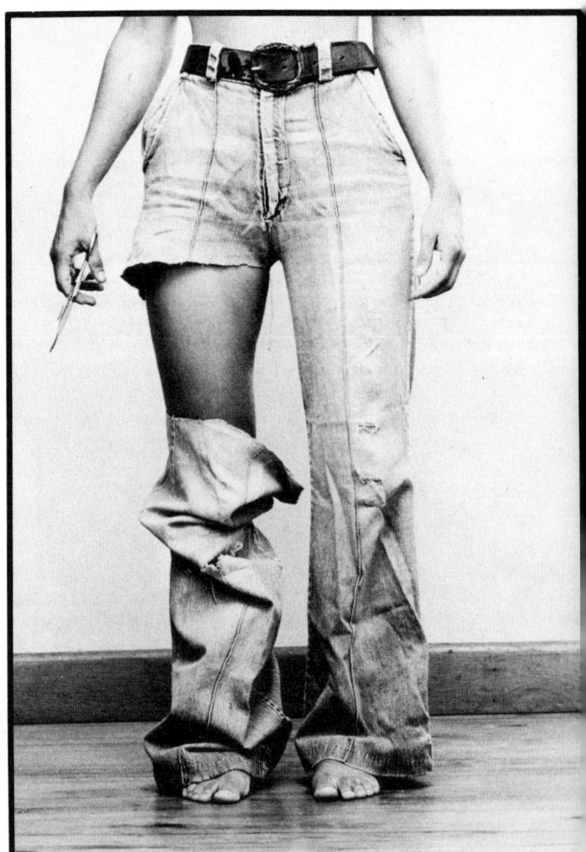

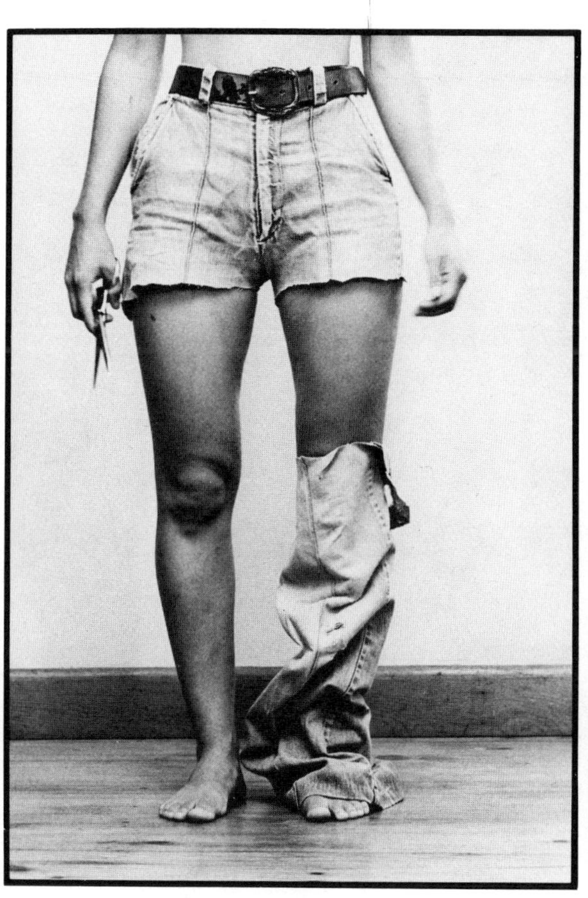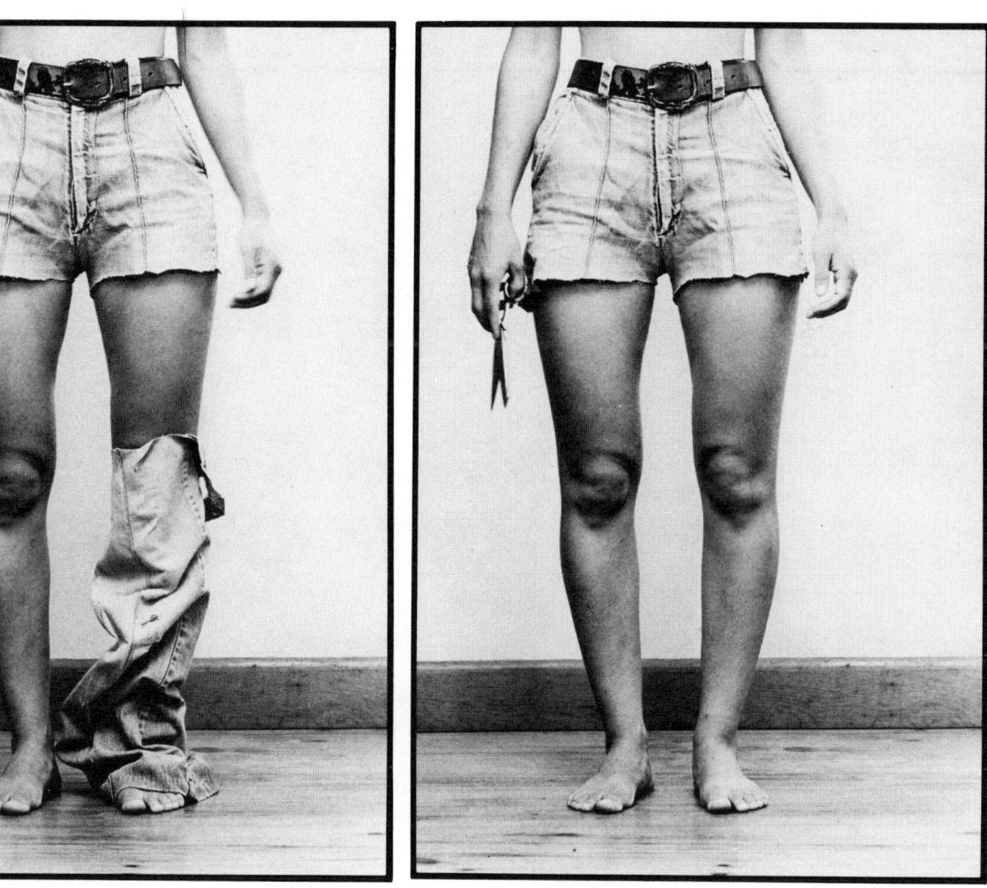

Recessive jeans

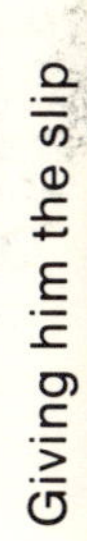

Giving him the slip

THE
ONE
MAINE SAVINGS BANK
12:00

THE
ONE
MAINE SAVINGS BANK
12:01

THE
ONE
MAINE SAVINGS BANK
12:02

A sign of the times

Meeting your match

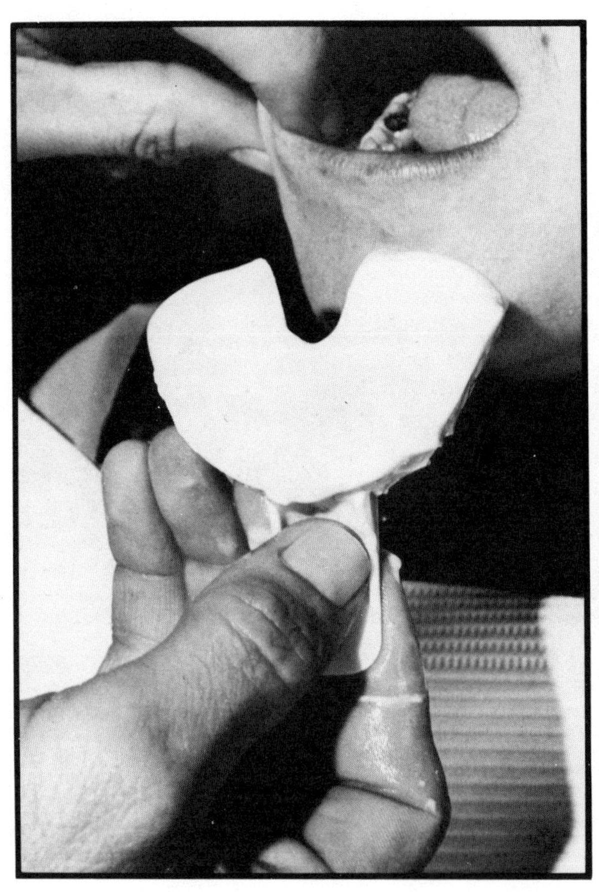  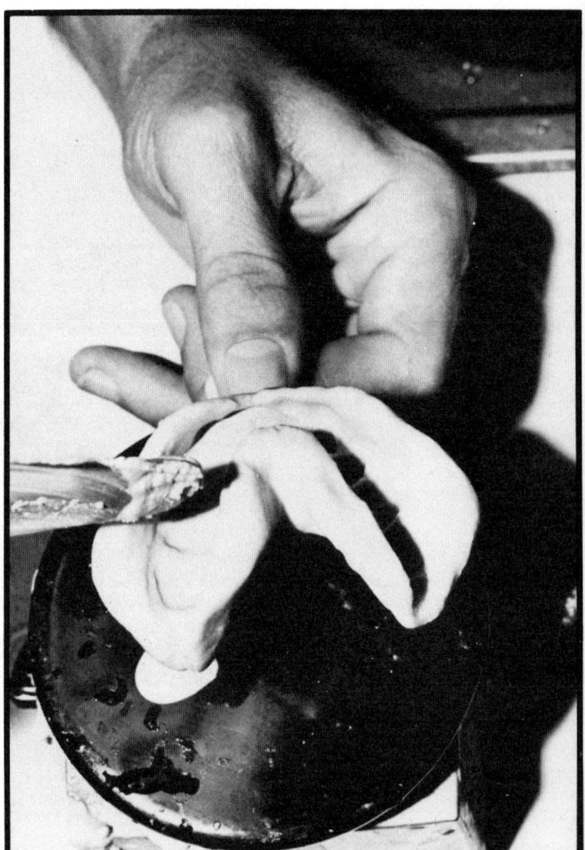

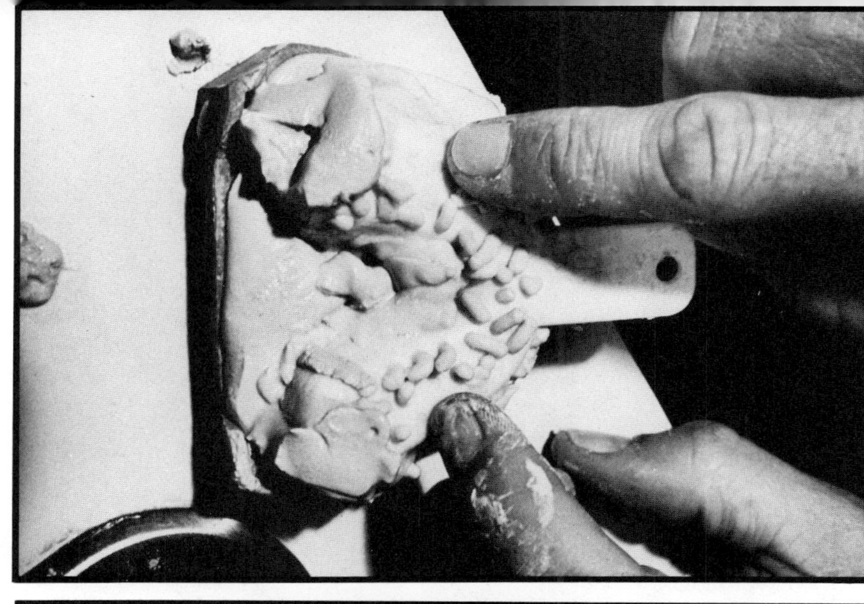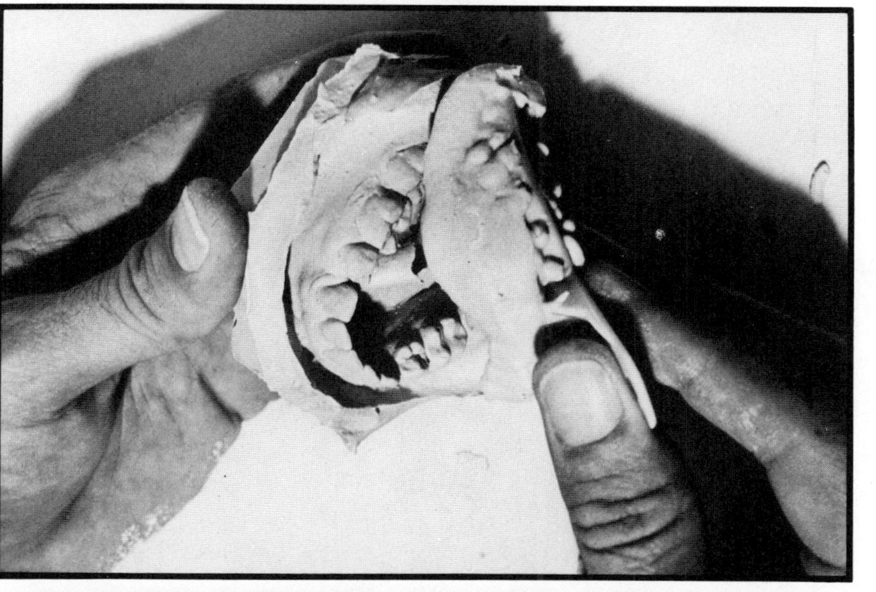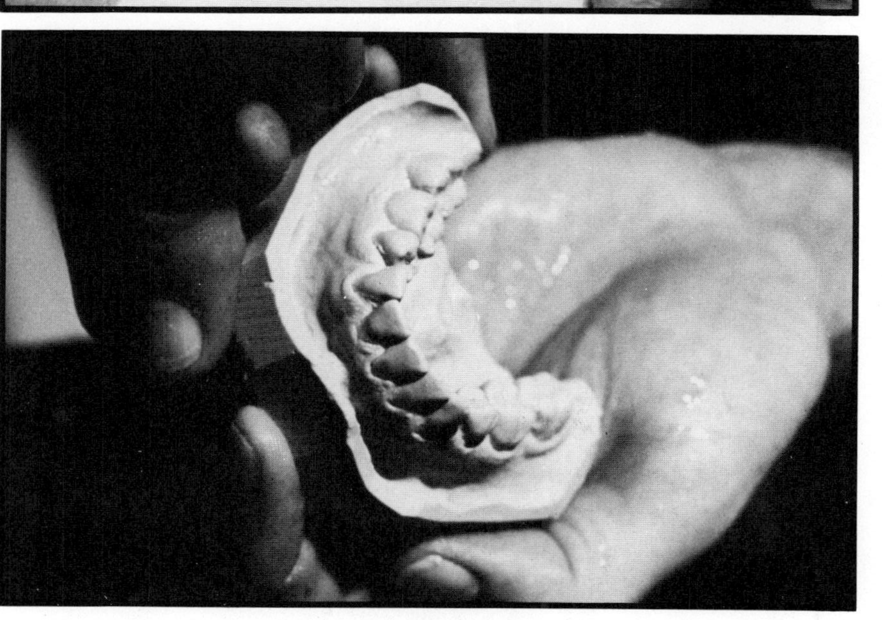

Making a lasting impression

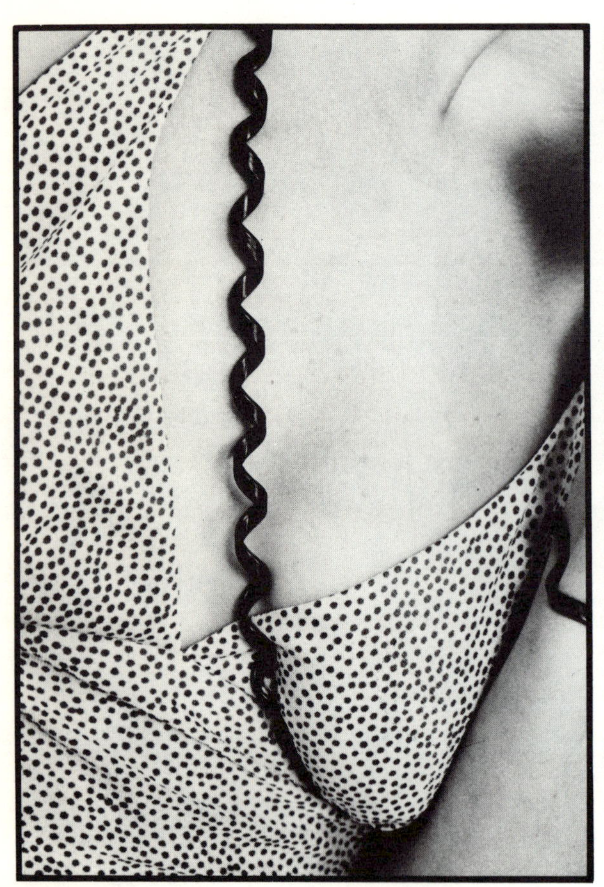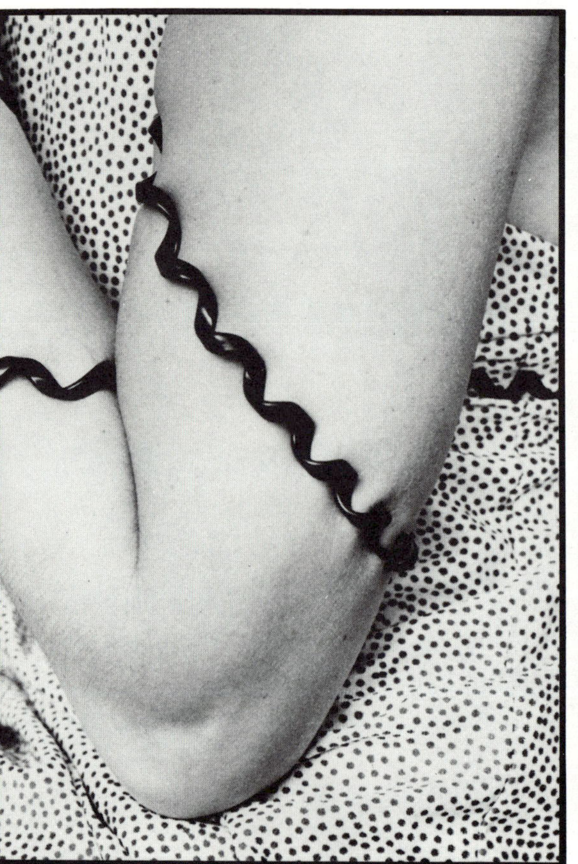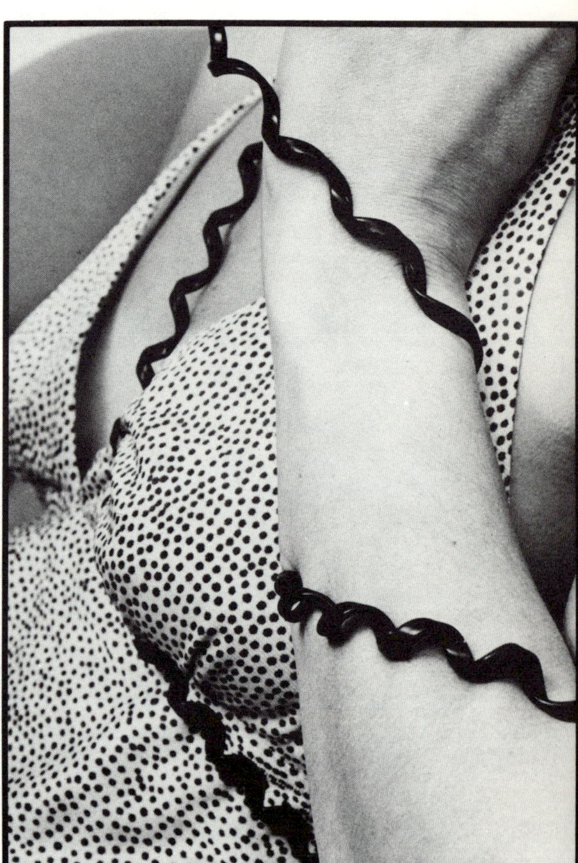

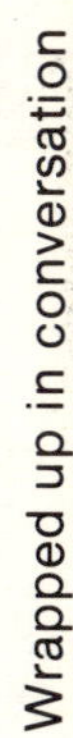

Wrapped up in conversation

She can't bare it anymore.

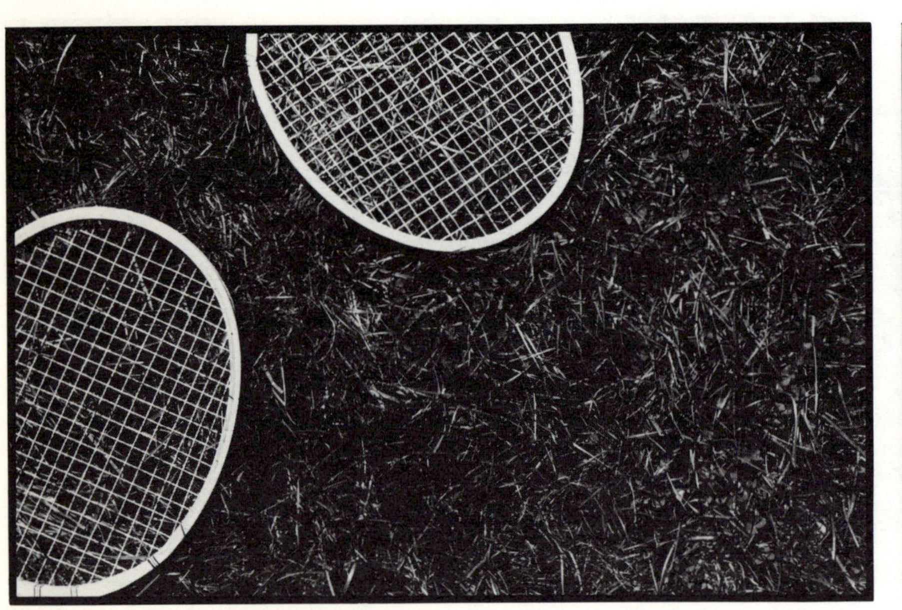

Birds of a feather flock together.

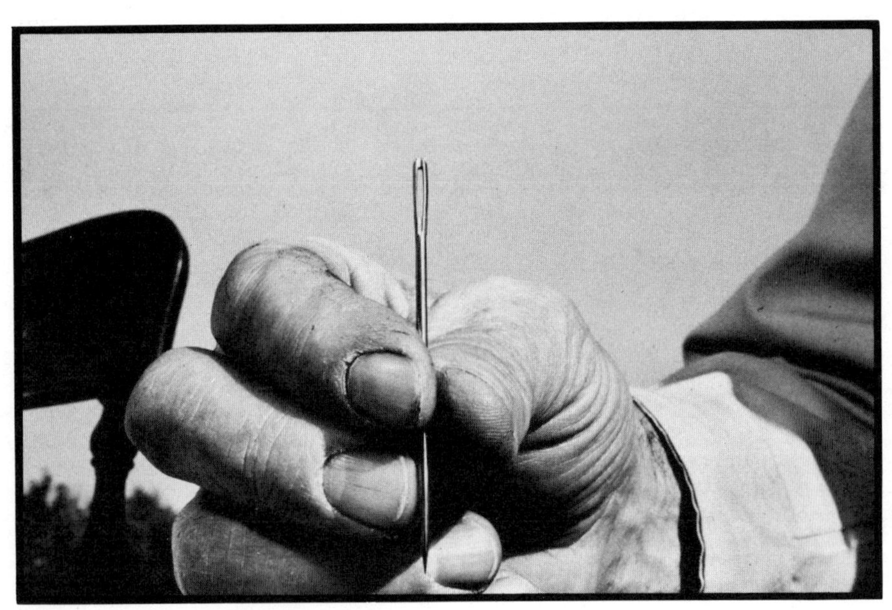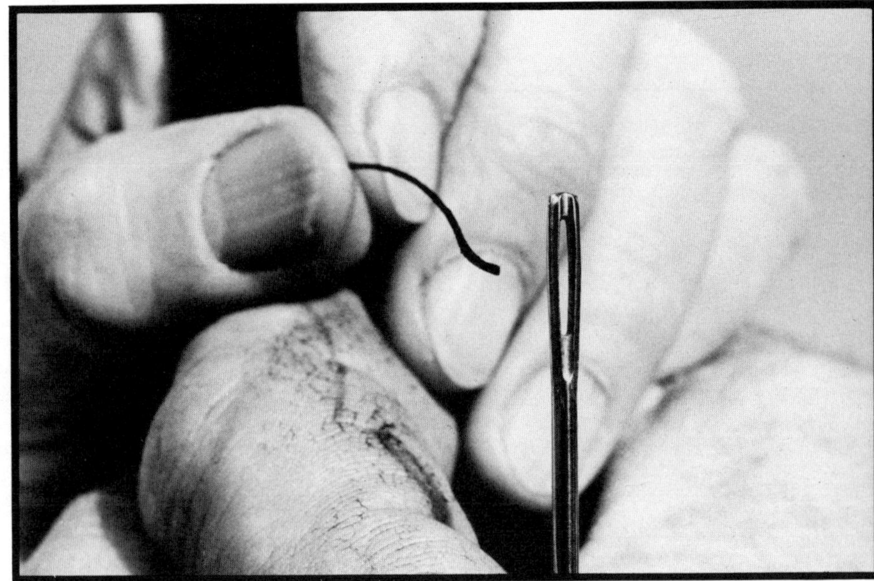

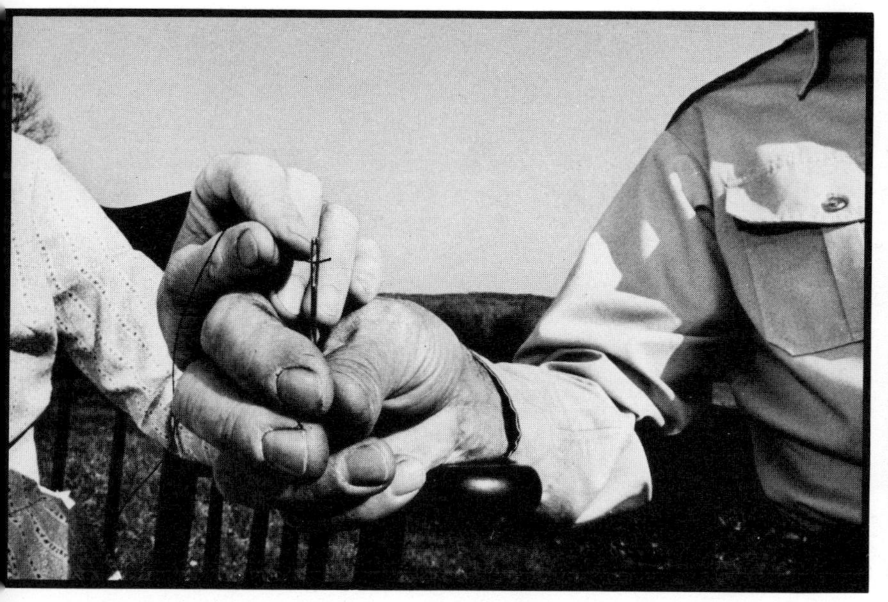

Catching his eye

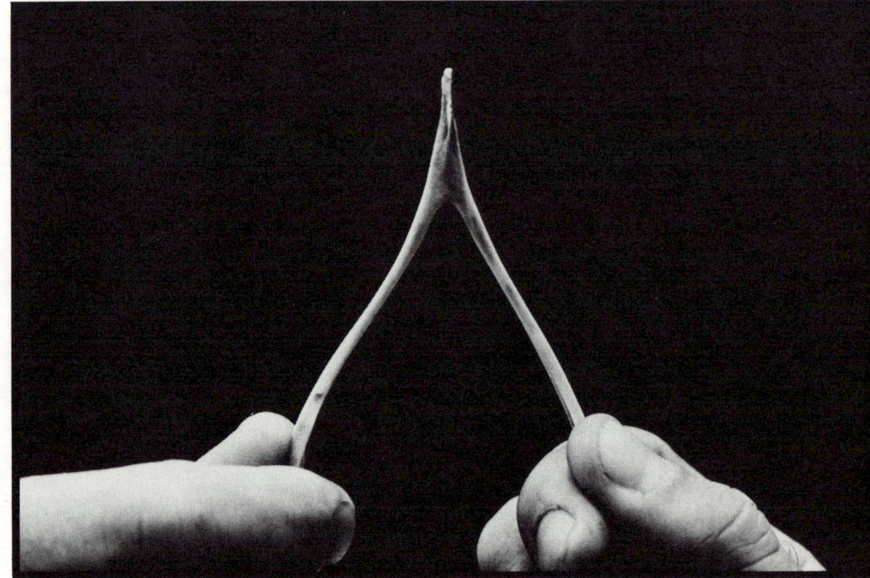

A bone of contention

Roll with the punches

Getting a load off his chest

If you don't like it—lump it.

Acknowledgments

I thank the following for their help and assistance and
participation in the photographing of this book:

Mom for her hand and Terry for making light of her work.

Sister Adele St. Pierre for forcing her habit.

John Schnell for playing it by ear.

Arthur "Jack" Goodwin and W. Edwin Loija for shooting the breeze.

The Kennebunk 5¢ to $ Store, Kennebunk, Maine, for their
best rules.

Tess Burke and Lee's Food Center, Sanford, Maine, for their
two heads, which were better than one.

David Rogers and his hog in the road.

Ken Cuneo, attorney at law, Rockland, Maine, for
closing the case.

Gregory Welch and the Portland (Maine) Museum of Art for making
a clean breast of it.

Nina Allen, who has appeal.

The Bag Restaurant, Portland, Maine, for being half in the bag.

Paul Guertin and the York County Savings Bank, Biddeford,
Maine, for playing it safe.

Seavey Printers, Portland, Maine, for letting me
lead their blind.

Russ Burleigh, of the Portland (Maine) Symphony Orchestra,
for taking a stand.

Pam Hale and her recessive jeans.

Priscilla Platt for giving husband David the slip.

The Maine Savings Bank, Saco, Maine, for providing me
with a sign of the times.

Marianna and Juliette Vall for meeting their match.

Dr. Carleton Mabee and his wife, Andrea, for making such
a lasting impression.

Eileen Kalikow, who's always wrapped up in conversation.

Robin Speno, who couldn't bare it anymore.

Officer Michael Breen, who wouldn't let her bare it anymore.

Jas Bailey Company, Portland, Maine, for their birdies.

Eleanor Loija for catching husband Edwin's eye.

Steve Bouchard, Tommy Butts, and Danny Butts—and their
bone of contention.

The Shawmut Inn, Kennebunkport, Maine, for rolling
with the punches.

James Hamblet and the University of Maine Athletic Department,
Portland, Maine, for getting a load off their chest.

Dad, who not only lumped it but also helped me out in more
ways than I can say thank you.

And all those others, too numerous to mention, but
they know who they are.

TECHNICAL DATA:
Cameras: Nikon F and F2/Pentax Spot Meter
Lenses: Nikkor 20mm, 28mm, 50mm, 55mm macro, 105mm, and 200mm
Film/Developer: Kodak Tri-X/Microdol-X
Printing Paper/
   Developer: Agfa Brovira, grades 3, 4, and 5/Dektol